CARNIVC

LIST

The Complete Ingredient list

and Food to Avoid for

Carnivore Diet

.

Harley W. Norman

Table of Contents

Introduction

In the bustling metropolis of Newhaven, where the pace of life never slows and the demand for quick, nutritious solutions is ever present, Julian, a seasoned nutritionist with a passion for transformative eating habits, decided to pen a masterpiece. His motivation was sparked by a realization that amidst the plethora of dietary advice and health trends, there was a significant gap in understanding and accessibility for those curious about or committed to a carnivore diet. Thus, was born "The Carnivore's Guide: Thriving on a Meat Based Diet," a book that promised not only to guide but also to enlighten.

Julian's journey into the world of carnivore dieting was not accidental. After witnessing countless clients struggle with conventional diets filled with complex carbohydrates, processed foods, and misleading "low-fat" options that led nowhere near their health goals, he ventured into the realms of ancestral eating patterns. His exploration was thorough, delving deep into scientific studies, historical dietary patterns, and the modern-day testimonials of those who had turned their health around by adopting a diet that many would deem unconventional.

"The Carnivore's Guide" was not just a food list. It was a manifesto, a beacon for those navigating the turbulent waters of dietary choices in a sea of misinformation. Julian knew his readers needed more than just recommendations; they sought understanding, simplicity, and effectiveness. Each chapter of the book was meticulously crafted, starting with an introduction that painted a vivid picture of the carnivore diet's origins, its principles, and the myriad of benefits it offered from weight loss and improved mental clarity to reduced inflammation and enhanced physical performance.

As the reader turned the pages, they were introduced to a world where food was not just fuel but medicine. The chapters were structured to provide a comprehensive guide on how to incorporate various meats, organ meats, fish, eggs, and animal fats into a daily routine, emphasizing the importance of quality and sourcing. Julian included a carefully curated list of recommended foods, detailed explanations on why certain items should be limited or avoided, and practical tips for navigating common challenges like dining out and managing social situations.

But what truly set "The Carnivore's Guide" apart was the narrative woven through the factual content. Julian shared stories of individuals who had transformed their lives through the carnivore diet, from overcoming chronic illnesses to achieving athletic feats once deemed impossible. These testimonials brought warmth and relatability to the pages, making the reader feel part of a community rather than a solitary journeyman.

In the concluding chapters, Julian addressed potential concerns and misconceptions, armed with evidence and empathetic advice. He acknowledged that while the carnivore diet might not be a universal solution, it offered a compelling option for those seeking to reset their relationship with food and their bodies.

As "The Carnivore's Guide" found its way into the hands of eager readers in Newhaven and beyond, it sparked conversations, debates, and, most importantly, changes. Those who had felt lost in the endless cycle of dieting found solace and success in the simplicity and clarity Julian's book provided. It wasn't just a diet book; it was a testament to the power of going back to the basics, listening to one's body, and embracing a diet that humanity thrived on for millennia.

Julian's decision to write "The Carnivore's Guide" was not just about selling a book; it was about offering a lifeline to those drowning in a sea of dietary confusion. It was an invitation to embark on a journey of discovery, transformation, and ultimately, liberation, from the chains of modern dietary dogmas. For anyone standing at the crossroads of dietary choices, "The Carnivore's Guide" wasn't just a book to buy; it was a new path to explore, promising a journey back to health, vitality, and simplicity.

Overview of the Carnivore Diet

Embarking on the carnivore diet journey is an exploration into a way of eating that prioritizes simplicity, nutrient density, and a profound connection to ancestral eating practices. This guide serves as a beacon for those seeking to navigate the world of a meat-based diet, offering clarity amidst the sea of dietary choices and misinformation. The essence of this guide is to equip you with the knowledge, strategies, and insights necessary to seamlessly integrate the carnivore diet into your lifestyle, whether you are a seasoned practitioner or a curious newcomer.

Start by familiarizing yourself with the fundamental principles of the carnivore diet, understanding its focus on animal products and the exclusion of plant-based foods. This foundation will help you grasp why certain foods are encouraged and others are avoided, illuminating the path towards making informed dietary choices that align with the carnivore philosophy.

The guide meticulously categorizes foods into recommended and delimited sections, providing a clear distinction between the diverse range of animal products that form the cornerstone of the diet. From the various types of meat, including beef, lamb, pork, and poultry, to organ meats, fish, eggs, and select dairy products, you'll find detailed descriptions of each food's nutritional benefits, preparation tips, and sourcing recommendations. Emphasis is placed on the importance of opting for grassfed, pasture raised, and wild caught sources to maximize the diet's health benefits.

Understanding the nuances of the diet is crucial, especially when it comes to fats and oils, where the guide advocates for animal-based fats like tallow and lard over processed vegetable oils. Similarly, the discussion around dairy products is nuanced, with an encouragement towards high fat options like butter and hard cheeses, while advising caution with processed dairy.

Beyond mere food lists, the guide delves into practical aspects of adopting a carnivore lifestyle. It addresses common challenges and provides solutions for dining out, dealing with social situations, and ensuring variety and enjoyment in your meals. Strategies for gradual adaptation are outlined for those transitioning from a more conventional diet, ensuring a smoother shift towards carnivore eating practices.

The guide doesn't shy away from addressing potential concerns and controversies surrounding the carnivore diet, offering evidence-based insights into its health impacts, debunking myths, and setting realistic expectations. It encourages readers to listen to their bodies, adapt the diet to their individual needs, and consult with healthcare professionals when necessary.

To enrich your journey, the guide includes additional resources like sample meal plans, shopping lists, designed to provide immediate, practical support. These tools aim to simplify the transition, making it easier to embrace the carnivore diet as a sustainable lifestyle choice rather than a temporary regimen.

Ultimately, this guide stands as more than just a collection of dos and don'ts; it's a comprehensive companion for your carnivore diet journey. It empowers you to make choices that align with your health goals, lifestyle preferences, and personal values, encouraging a deeper understanding and appreciation of this primal way of eating. Through education, practical advice, and supportive resources, it aims to demystify the carnivore diet, making it accessible and enjoyable for all who wish to explore its potential benefits.

Benefits and Considerations

The carnivore diet, centered exclusively on animal products, offers a unique approach to nutrition that diverges significantly from conventional dietary guidelines. Its proponents highlight a range of benefits, from weight loss and improved metabolic health to enhanced mental clarity and simplicity in meal planning. Yet, it's critical to weigh these potential advantages against considerations and possible challenges associated with such a restrictive dietary pattern.

Among the touted benefits, many individuals report significant weight loss when adopting a carnivore diet, likely due to its high protein content and the satiety that comes from consuming fats and proteins, which may reduce overall calorie intake. This diet's emphasis on whole, unprocessed animal foods can lead to a reduction in sugar and carbohydrate consumption, helping to stabilize blood sugar levels and improve insulin sensitivity, potentially offering benefits for those with diabetes or metabolic syndrome.

Improved digestive health is another commonly reported advantage, as the elimination of fiber rich plant foods can alleviate symptoms in some individuals with digestive disorders such as IBS or bloating. The high intake of nutrient dense organ meats and fatty fish also provides essential vitamins and minerals, including vitamin B12, iron, zinc, and omega3 fatty acids, which are crucial for brain health, immune function, and overall wellbeing.

Mental clarity and increased energy levels are anecdotal benefits shared by those on the carnivore diet. Some suggest that stabilizing blood sugar levels eliminates the highs and lows associated with carbohydrate consumption, leading to better focus and sustained energy throughout the day.

Despite these potential benefits, there are several considerations to keep in mind. The restrictive nature of the carnivore diet raises concerns about nutritional deficiencies, particularly for vitamins C and E, fiber, and certain antioxidants found predominantly in fruits and vegetables. There's also the potential impact on heart health due to the high intake of saturated fats and cholesterol found in red meat, though recent research challenges the direct link between saturated fat consumption and cardiovascular disease.

Environmental and ethical considerations are paramount for some individuals, given the significant environmental footprint associated with high levels of meat consumption. Additionally, sourcing high-quality, grassfed, and organic meats, which are often recommended to maximize health benefits, can be more expensive and less accessible for many people.

The long-term effects of the carnivore diet are not well documented, and most health professionals caution against extreme dietary patterns that eliminate whole groups of foods. Transitioning to such a diet may also lead to initial side effects, including fatigue, headaches, and constipation, as the body adjusts to a lack of dietary carbohydrates and fiber.

Choosing to follow a carnivore diet requires careful consideration and possibly consultation with a healthcare provider, particularly for individuals with existing health conditions. It may be beneficial for some, especially as a temporary elimination diet to identify food sensitivities or for those who have not found success with more conventional dietary approaches. However, it's important to consider the potential risks and ensure that the diet is nutritionally complete, possibly through the use of supplements and a focus on variety within the allowed foods to minimize nutritional deficiencies.

Chapter 1: Essential Proteins

Type of Meat	Recommended Carnivore Foods	Food Limit or Avoid
Beef	Grassfed and grass finished beef for higher omega3 fatty acids and vitamins. Varied cuts like ribeye, sirloin, and brisket to balance fat and protein intake. Organ meats such as liver for a nutrient dense option.	Processed beef products like sausages and burgers with added fillers or preservatives. Beef jerky with added sugars or artificial ingredients.
Lamb	Grassfed lamb for its rich flavor and high nutrient profile, including iron and zinc. Lamb chops and leg of lamb are excellent for roasting or grilling. Lamb liver and heart as nutrient rich organ options.	Lamb products that are heavily processed or contain additives. Lamb sausages or minced lamb with added ingredients that stray from the carnivore diet principles.

Type of Meat	Recommended Carnivore Foods	Food Limit or Avoid
Pork	Pasture raised pork for a healthier fat profile. Pork chops, tenderloin, and shoulder cuts for diversity in meals. Pork belly provides a high fat option for those focusing on increased fat intake.	Processed pork products like bacon and ham that contain nitrates, sugars, and other additives. Pork rinds that may contain unhealthy cooking oils or flavorings.
Chicken	Free-range or organic chicken to avoid antibiotics and hormones. A mix of dark and light meat, such as thighs and breasts, to balance fat and lean protein. Chicken liver as a low-fat but nutrient dense option.	Chicken products that are breaded or prevaricated in sauces with sugar and artificial ingredients. Deli chicken slices that may contain preservatives.
Turkey	Organic or wild turkey for a lean protein source. Ground turkey for homemade burgers or meatballs, ensuring no fillers are added. Turkey	Processed turkey products, including turkey bacon and deli slices with added sugars and fillers. Precooked turkey products with preservatives

Type of Meat	Recommended Carnivore Foods	Food Limit or Avoid
	organs like liver and heart for variety in nutrient intake.	and artificial flavorings.

Chapter 2: Seafood and Fish

This content is tailored to individuals following or considering a carnivore diet, highlighting the benefits and considerations of including these types of seafood in their diet.

Seafood/Fish Type	Carnivore Diet Recommendation	Nutritional Highlights	Preparation Tips and Considerations
Salmon	Highly Recommended (Wild Caught)	Rich in omega3 fatty acids, high-quality protein, selenium, and vitamins B12 and D.	opt for grilled, baked, or steamed salmon to preserve its nutritional value. Avoid adding breading or deep-frying. Wild caught salmon is preferred for its lower contaminant levels and higher omega3 content compared to farmed salmon.

Seafood/Fish Type	Carnivore Diet Recommendation	Nutritional Highlights	Preparation Tips and Considerations
Mackerel	Highly Recommended (Wild Caught)	Excellent source of omega3 fatty acids, vitamin D, selenium, and protein. Mackerel is known for its rich, oily flesh.	Smoked or grilled mackerel are ideal preparation methods. Mackerel can be enjoyed as a steak or fillet. It's important to ensure its wild caught to avoid high mercury levels that can be present in larger fish.
Sardines	Highly Recommended (Wild Caught)	Packed with omega3 fatty acids, calcium (from bones), vitamin D,	Sardines can be consumed canned or fresh. For those on a carnivore diet, it's best to consume sardines in water

Seafood/Fish Type	Carnivore Diet Recommendation	Nutritional Highlights	Preparation Tips and Considerations
		and protein. Sardines are a nutrient dense small fish.	or olive oil rather than those in sauces or marinades. Grilled or baked sardines are a nutritious option.
Tuna	Recommended with Caution (Wild Caught)	High in omega3 fatty acids and protein. Tuna is a versatile fish but varies widely in mercury content based on the species.	Fresh tuna steaks are best enjoyed grilled or seared. Limit intake of larger tuna species like albacore, which have higher mercury levels. opt for skipjack or light canned tuna for lower mercury options.

General Carnivore Diet Tips for Seafood and Fish:

- **Wild Caught Fish:** Emphasized for their lower levels of pollutants and higher omega3 fatty acid content. Wild caught fish align well with the carnivore diet's focus on natural, unprocessed foods.
- **Food Limit or Avoid:** Breaded or deep-fried seafood should be limited or avoided due to their added carbohydrates and unhealthy fats, which are not compliant with the carnivore diet principles. These preparation methods can also diminish the nutritional value of the fish.

Incorporating wild caught salmon, mackerel, sardines, and tuna into a carnivore diet provides an excellent source of essential nutrients, including omega3 fatty acids, high-quality protein, and various vitamins and minerals. By choosing appropriate preparation methods and being mindful of the types of fish consumed, individuals can enjoy the health benefits of seafood while adhering to the carnivore diet guidelines.

Chapter 3: Organ Meats

When embarking on a carnivore diet, an all meat and animal products regimen, it's crucial to focus on the nutritional value and variety of the foods consumed. Organ meats, also known as offal, are among the most nutrient dense foods you can include in your diet. Here's a closer look at the benefits of liver, heart, kidneys, and brain in relation to a carnivore diet, along with recommendations for other carnivore friendly foods and considerations for foods to limit or avoid due to overconsumption concerns.

Nutrient Dense Organs on the Carnivore Diet

Organ Meat	Nutrients Provided	Benefits
Liver	Vitamins A, B12, B6, Iron, Choline, Copper, Folate	The liver is often considered nature's multivitamin. It supports energy levels, brain health, and the immune system.
Heart	CoQ10, Vitamins, Iron, Selenium	Heart meat is rich in CoQ10, crucial for energy production and cardiovascular health.

Organ Meat	Nutrients Provided	Benefits
Kidneys	Selenium, Iron, Copper, Zinc, Vitamins	Kidneys support detoxification processes in the body and boost the immune system.
Brain	Omega3 Fatty Acids, Cholesterol, Selenium	Brain tissue is high in omega3 fatty acids, which support brain health and cognitive function.

Recommended Carnivore Foods

Alongside organ meats, here are other nutrient dense foods to incorporate into a carnivore diet:

Food Type	Examples	Nutrient Benefits
Muscle Meats	Beef, Pork, Lamb, Chicken	Primary source of protein and B vitamins.
Fatty Fish	Salmon, Mackerel, Sardines	High in omega3 fatty acids, vitamin D, and selenium.
Eggs	Whole eggs	Rich in choline, vitamins B12 and D, and selenium.
Dairy	Cheese, Butter, Heavy Cream	Source of calcium, vitamin D, and fatty acids.

Food Limit or Avoid: Overconsumption Concerns

While a carnivore diet emphasizes meat and animal products, certain foods should be consumed in moderation to avoid potential health issues related to overconsumption:

Food to Limit/Avoid	Concerns	Recommended Action
Processed Meats	High in sodium and preservatives, which may increase the risk of heart disease and certain cancers.	Limit intake and choose fresh, unprocessed meats when possible.
Excessive Fatty Meats	High saturated fat intake can impact cholesterol levels and heart health for some individuals.	Balance with leaner meats and consider incorporating fatty fish for healthier fats.
High Intake of Certain Organs	Consuming large amounts of liver can lead to vitamin A toxicity. High intake of kidneys may increase uric acid, potentially leading to gout.	Consume organ meats in moderation, balancing with muscle meats and other animal products.

Incorporating a variety of organ meats and other animal products can ensure a balanced intake of essential nutrients while adhering to a carnivore diet. However, it's important to balance your diet and monitor your health, as individual nutritional needs and tolerances can vary. Consulting with a healthcare provider or a nutritionist specializing in carnivore diets can provide personalized advice and adjustments based on your health goals and dietary needs.

Chapter 4: Fats and Oils

The carnivore diet emphasizes consumption of meat and animal products while eliminating plant-based foods. Within this diet, the quality and sources of fats are crucial, as they provide energy, support cell growth, and help in the absorption of fat-soluble vitamins. Below is a comprehensive table that outlines recommended animal fats, including tallow, lard, and duck fat, and advises on which fats to limit or avoid, specifically industrial seed and vegetable oils.

Category	Recommended Carnivore Foods	Food to Limit or Avoid
Animal Fats (Highly Recommended)	**Tallow:** Derived from beef or mutton fat, tallow is rich in vitamins A, D, E, and K. It's ideal for cooking at high temperatures due to its high smoke point. **Lard:** Rendered pork fat, lard is a source of vitamin D and monounsaturated fats. It's suitable for baking and frying. **Duck	**Industrial Seed and Vegetable Oils:** These oils, such as canola, soybean, corn, and sunflower oil, are highly processed and often contain high levels of omega6 fatty acids, which can lead to inflammation when consumed in excess. It's recommended to

Category	Recommended Carnivore Foods	Food to Limit or Avoid
	Fat: Extracted from duck skin, it's known for its rich flavor and is high in monounsaturated fats, making it great for roasting and sautéing.	avoid these oils on a carnivore diet due to their processing methods and potential health impacts.

Key Points on Tallow, Lard, and Duck Fat in the Carnivore Diet:

- **Tallow** is highly valued in the carnivore diet for its nutrient profile and versatility in cooking. It can be used for frying, sautéing, and even as a spread. Its high smoke point makes it one of the safest fats for high temperature cooking.

- **Lard** is celebrated not only for its culinary uses but also for its nutritional benefits. It's particularly rich in vitamin D, which is essential for bone health and immune function. Lard can be used in a variety of culinary applications, from frying to creating flaky pastries.

- **Duck Fat** offers a unique flavor profile and is a favorite for enhancing the taste of roasted vegetables (for those who include some plant-based foods in their diet) and meats. Its high content of monounsaturated fats makes it a heart healthy option within the carnivore diet.

Recommendations:

- **Prioritize Animal Fats:** On a carnivore diet, prioritize animal fats like tallow, lard, and duck fat for their nutrient density and health benefits.
- **Limit Industrial Oils:** Avoid industrial seed and vegetable oils due to their inflammatory properties and the potential for negative health impacts.
- **Variety and Balance:** Incorporate a variety of animal fats to ensure a balanced intake of different fatty acids and fat-soluble vitamins.

By focusing on nutrient dense animal fats and avoiding processed oils, individuals following a carnivore diet can optimize their health and wellbeing. Tallow, lard, and duck fat not only offer exceptional nutritional benefits but also enhance the flavor of carnivore diet meals, making them enjoyable and satisfying.

Chapter 5: Dairy Products

The carnivore diet emphasizes the consumption of animal products and eliminates plant-based foods. Dairy products, particularly those high in fat, can be included but should be chosen wisely to align with the diet's principles. Here's a detailed overview of how butter, ghee, and hard cheeses fit into the carnivore diet, including a list of recommended foods and those to avoid.

Table 1: Dairy Products on the Carnivore Diet

Category	Recommended Foods	Foods to Limit or Avoid
Butter	Grassfed butter	Margarine
		Butter substitutes
Ghee	Organic, grassfed ghee	Vegetable ghee
Hard Cheeses	Aged cheddar	Processed cheese slices
	Parmesan	Cheese products with additives
	Gouda	
General Guidance	High Fat Dairy Products	Low-fat and Processed Dairy
	Heavy cream	Skim milk
	Full fat sour cream	Low-fat yogurt

Category	Recommended Foods	Foods to Limit or Avoid
	Full fat Greek yogurt (limited)	Low-fat cheese
		Dairy with added sugars

Recommendations and Considerations:

- **Butter and Ghee:** Both are excellent sources of healthy fats on the carnivore diet, ideal for cooking and enhancing flavor. They are rich in fat-soluble vitamins and conjugated linoleic acid (CLA), which can offer anti-inflammatory benefits. opt for products from grassfed animals for higher nutritional content.

- **Hard Cheeses:** These are a good source of protein, fat, calcium, and other minerals. They are less likely to cause issues for people with lactose intolerance due to their lower lactose content. However, it's important to select varieties without added flavors or preservatives.

- **High Fat Dairy:** Emphasizes the importance of consuming full fat dairy products to maintain high energy levels and nutritional adequacy. High fat dairy is also more satiating, which can help control hunger and support weight management.

- **Low-fat and Processed Dairy:** These products often contain added sugars, flavors, and preservatives, which can disrupt the balance of the carnivore diet. Additionally, the removal of fat reduces the vitamin and mineral content of dairy products, diminishing their nutritional value.

Incorporating high fat dairy products like butter, ghee, and hard cheeses into a carnivore diet can provide essential nutrients, enhance flavor, and increase satiety. It is crucial to choose products that are as natural and minimally processed as possible to align with the carnivore diet's principles. Avoid low-fat and processed dairy products, as they often contain undesirable additives and lower nutritional value.

Chapter 6: Eggs

The Carnivore Diet emphasizes consuming animal products exclusively, with a focus on meats and foods derived directly from animals. This dietary approach often prioritizes foods that are rich in protein and fats while eliminating carbohydrates, including those from plants. Within this context, whole eggs are an essential component of the Carnivore Diet due to their nutritional profile, versatility, and alignment with the diet's principles. Below is a detailed table outlining the role of whole eggs in the Carnivore Diet, including recommendations on consumption and notes on egg substitutes and products with additives.

Category	Details
Recommended Carnivore Foods	**Whole Eggs**
Details	Whole eggs are highly recommended on the Carnivore Diet as they are a complete source of protein, containing all nine essential amino acids necessary for human health. They are also rich in vitamins (including Vitamin D, B12, and A), minerals (such as selenium and zinc), and healthy fats, including omega3 fatty acids. Eggs from pasture raised chickens are

Category	Details
	preferred for their higher nutrient content.
Serving Suggestions	Whole eggs can be consumed daily, with the quantity adjusted according to individual energy needs, activity levels, and specific health goals. They can be prepared in various ways, including boiling, frying, poaching, or scrambling, with minimal or no additives.
Foods to Limit or Avoid	**Egg Substitutes and Products with Additives**
Details	Egg substitutes and egg products containing additives, such as those designed to lower cholesterol or those enriched with additional vitamins, are not recommended on the Carnivore Diet. These products often contain nonanimal derived ingredients and additives that the diet advises against, such as vegetable oils, artificial colors, or flavors.

Category	Details
Examples of Avoided Products	Liquid egg products with added flavors or preservatives, powdered eggs with additional ingredients for color or texture, and any egg-based product that includes plant derived additives or preservatives should be avoided.

Key Takeaways

- **Nutritional Value**: Whole eggs are a nutrient dense food perfectly aligned with the Carnivore Diet's emphasis on animal-based nutrition. They provide essential proteins, fats, vitamins, and minerals.
- **Dietary Role**: They serve as a versatile and convenient food item that can be incorporated into daily meals, providing both satiety and nutritional benefits.
- **Limitations**: While whole eggs are encouraged, any form of egg substitutes or products with nonanimal derived additives are to be avoided to maintain the diet's strict adherence to animal-based foods.

Whole eggs represent a cornerstone food item within the Carnivore Diet, celebrated for their comprehensive nutritional profile and alignment with the diet's focus on high-quality animal products. When following this diet, individuals are advised to consume whole eggs in their most natural form, avoiding processed egg products and substitutes to stay true to the diet's principles.

Chapter 7: Beverages

The carnivore diet emphasizes consuming animal products exclusively, which significantly limits the variety of beverages considered acceptable. Below is a detailed table highlighting recommended beverages, as well as those to limit or avoid entirely within the context of the carnivore diet.

This guide aims to offer clarity for individuals adhering to or considering this diet, especially in terms of what drinks can complement such a lifestyle without compromising its principles.

Category	Beverage	Description	Considerations
Recommended	Water	Pure, unflavored water is the most recommended beverage in the carnivore diet for hydration without adding any carbs or sugars.	Ensures hydration without breaking the diet's strict noncard rule. Drinking adequate water is essential for overall health.

Category	Beverage	Description	Considerations
	Bone Broth	A nutrient rich liquid made by simmering bones and connective tissues of animals. Provides minerals and collagen.	Supports joint health, digestion, and provides essential nutrients that may be missing from a strictly carnivorous diet.
Limit or avoid	Alcoholic Beverages	Alcohol is generally advised against on the carnivore diet due to its potential to disrupt metabolism and health benefits.	Can interfere with weight loss, contribute to inflammation, and disrupt sleep patterns.
	Sugary Drinks	This includes sodas, fruit juices, and any beverages with added sugars.	Sugary drinks can spike insulin levels, leading to health issues and deviation from the

Category	Beverage	Description	Considerations
		They are not compliant with the carnivore diet.	diet's goals.

Key Points to Remember:

- **Water** should be your primary beverage choice to maintain hydration levels effectively. It's crucial for metabolic processes and overall health.

- **Bone Broth** is not only allowed but recommended for its nutrient profile, which can complement the high protein nature of the carnivore diet by providing minerals and other beneficial compounds.

- **Alcoholic Beverages** should be consumed with caution if at all. While some may choose to include them in moderation, it's important to recognize their potential to undermine diet goals and health improvements.

- **Sugary Drinks** are strictly off-limits as they are antithetical to the core principles of the carnivore diet. Their consumption can lead to sugar spikes and crashes, undermining the diet's benefits and potentially leading to cravings for other noncompliant foods.

Sticking to water and bone broth aligns best with the principles of the carnivore diet, ensuring that you stay hydrated and receive essential nutrients without introducing unwanted sugars or alcohol. These guidelines aim to support those on the carnivore diet in making beverage choices that align with their health and dietary goals.

Chapter 8: Seasonings and Additives

The carnivore diet primarily emphasizes the consumption of animal products and typically excludes plant-based foods. However, to cater to individual taste preferences and nutritional needs while maintaining the diet's principles, minimal use of certain natural spices and seasonings can be incorporated.

It's crucial to distinguish between recommended seasonings that can enhance the diet without detracting from its core philosophy and those additives, processed sauces, and condiments that should be limited or avoided due to their potential to introduce unwanted carbohydrates, sugars, and artificial ingredients.

Category	Recommended for Minimal Use (Natural Spices)	Food Limit or Avoid (Processed Sauces and Condiments)
Salt and Pepper	Unrefined Sea Salt Himalayan Pink Salt Black Pepper (in moderation)	Iodized Table Salt (due to potential additives)

Category	Recommended for Minimal Use (Natural Spices)	Food Limit or Avoid (Processed Sauces and Condiments)
Herbs and Spices (Fresh/Dried)	Garlic Powder (in moderation) Onion Powder (in moderation) Fresh Herbs like Rosemary, Thyme (in moderation)	Mixed Spice Blends (due to potential sugar and additives) Spice Mixes with MSG or Artificial Flavors
Fats and Oils	Animal Fats (Tallow, Lard) for cooking	Vegetable Oils (Canola, Soybean, etc.) Margarine and other processed fats
Vinegars	Apple Cider Vinegar (unfiltered, in moderation)	Balsamic Vinegar (contains sugars) Flavored Vinegars (due to added sugars and artificial flavors)
Sauces and Condiments	Homemade Bone Broth (as a base for sauces, no added sugars)	Ketchup (high in sugars) BBQ Sauce (high in sugars and additives) Most Commercial Salad

Category	Recommended for Minimal Use (Natural Spices)	Food Limit or Avoid (Processed Sauces and Condiments)
		Dressings (due to vegetable oils and sugars)
Sweeteners	None recommended	All forms of Sugar (white, brown, etc.) Artificial Sweeteners (aspartame, sucralose, etc.) Natural Sweeteners (honey, maple syrup, etc.)
Other Additives	None recommended	Food Colorings Preservatives Artificial Flavors Texturizers and Emulsifiers

Guidelines for Minimal Use of Natural Spices:

- The inclusion of natural spices should be moderate and mindful, ensuring they do not become a central part of the diet but rather a means to enhance the flavor of animal products without introducing significant plant matter.

- Listening to your body's response to spices is crucial, as some individuals may experience inflammatory reactions or digestive issues even with minimal plant product inclusion.

Rationale for Avoiding Processed Sauces and Condiments:

- Processed sauces and condiments often contain high levels of sugars, unhealthy fats, and artificial additives that can compromise the health benefits sought through the carnivore diet.
- These products can also introduce unwanted carbs, disrupting the metabolic advantages of a carnivore diet, such as maintained insulin sensitivity and ketosis.

While the carnivore diet is restrictive by nature, the thoughtful inclusion of certain natural spices can accommodate personal preferences without detracting from the diet's benefits. Conversely, vigilance against processed additives and condiments is crucial to maintain the diet's integrity and health outcomes.

Chapter 9: Implementing the Carnivore Diet

Planning Your Carnivore Diet

Implementing the carnivore diet successfully requires thoughtful preparation and understanding of the food list central to this dietary regimen. At its core, the carnivore diet consists of animal products exclusively, eschewing plant-based foods. This approach emphasizes the consumption of meat, fish, eggs, and certain dairy products while prioritizing nutrient density and simplicity in eating habits.

To start, focusing on the quality of meat is crucial. Grass-fed and pasture-raised meats are recommended for their higher nutritional profiles, including better omega-3 to omega-6 fatty acid ratios and more abundant vitamins A and E. Organ meats, such as liver, heart, and kidneys, are particularly nutrient-dense and provide a wide array of vitamins and minerals that are essential for optimal health. Incorporating a variety of meats ensures a broad spectrum of nutrients. Beef, lamb, pork, chicken, and game meats are staples, with fish and seafood offering vital omega-3 fatty acids.

Eggs are another cornerstone of the carnivore diet, offering high-quality protein and fats, vitamins, and minerals. They can be consumed in any form, providing both versatility and nutritional benefits. For those who tolerate dairy, high-fat products like butter, cream, and hard cheeses can be included for extra fat sources, though it's important to monitor individual responses to dairy.

Hydration is primarily maintained through water consumption, and bone broth is another excellent source of nutrients and hydration, providing minerals and amino acids that support digestive health and joint health.

The carnivore diet simplifies meal planning and preparation. Meals are centered around a single main ingredient—meat—and require minimal seasoning, focusing on natural spices in moderation if desired. Cooking methods can vary, with grilling, roasting, and slow cooking being popular choices that enhance flavor and tenderness.

Transitioning to a carnivore diet may involve an adaptation period. Some individuals experience flu-like symptoms as their body adjusts to ketosis, a state where fat is primarily used for energy in the absence of carbohydrates. It's important to allow time for adjustment, stay hydrated, and perhaps increase salt intake to manage electrolyte balance during this phase.

The exclusion of processed foods, sugars, and plant-based foods aims to reduce inflammation, improve digestion, and support metabolic health. Advocates often report improvements in energy levels, mental clarity, and weight management. However, it's essential to listen to the body's signals and consider consulting with a healthcare provider to ensure nutritional needs are met, particularly for individuals with specific health conditions.

In summary, planning a carnivore diet involves choosing high-quality animal products, incorporating variety for nutritional balance, simplifying meal preparation, and being mindful of the body's adaptation process. This diet promotes a return to a more natural, less processed way of eating, focusing on the nutritional richness of animal foods.

Tips for Eating Out and Social Events

Navigating eating out and attending social events while adhering to the carnivore diet can be challenging, given its strict emphasis on animal products and exclusion of plant-based foods. However, with strategic planning and communication, it's possible to maintain this dietary approach without sacrificing social engagements or dining experiences. When eating at restaurants, opting for steak houses, barbecue joints, or places known for their meat-centric menus can make it easier to find options that fit within the carnivore diet. It's beneficial to review menus online before visiting to identify suitable dishes, and don't hesitate to ask for modifications, such as substituting side dishes with extra portions of animal-based foods like eggs or a side of bacon.

Direct communication with the chef or server about dietary preferences can also ensure meals are prepared without added ingredients that deviate from the carnivore lifestyle, like sauces and dressings rich in sugars and vegetable oils. Requesting that your dish be cooked in animal fat or butter instead of vegetable oils is another way to stick closer to the diet's guidelines. In social settings or events where food is served, eating a carnivore-friendly meal beforehand can reduce temptation and make it easier to navigate the available options. Bringing your own dishes to share, when possible, ensures there's something you can eat, and it introduces others to the carnivore way of eating.

For those strictly adhering to the diet, it's important to remember that flexibility in social situations may not always align perfectly with the carnivore diet's principles. In such cases, focusing on the most minimally processed animal foods available can help maintain adherence without completely isolating oneself from social dining experiences. Beverages can also pose a challenge, but sticking to water, sparkling water, or even bringing your own bone broth can provide alternatives to sugary or alcoholic drinks often present at social gatherings.

Lastly, being open about your dietary choices can sometimes lead to supportive conversations and a better understanding among peers and hosts. While it's crucial to stay true to one's dietary convictions, maintaining a balanced perspective on social interactions and the primary goals of your diet can help navigate these situations with less stress and more enjoyment. Emphasizing the positive aspects of the carnivore diet, such as its simplicity and how it makes you feel, rather than focusing solely on the restrictions, can also foster a more inclusive atmosphere at social events.

Chapter 10: Challenges and Solutions

Common Challenges When Starting

Adapting to the carnivore diet involves significant dietary changes that can present challenges for those new to this way of eating. One common hurdle is the initial adjustment period, often referred to as the adaptation phase. During this time, individuals may experience flu-like symptoms, including headaches, fatigue, and irritability, as their bodies shift from using carbohydrates to fats as the primary energy source. To mitigate these effects, it's crucial to stay hydrated and ensure adequate salt intake, as the diet naturally leads to a reduction in water retention and electrolytes.

Another challenge is nutrient diversity, given the diet's exclusive focus on animal products. Concerns about potential deficiencies in vitamins and minerals typically obtained from plant foods can be addressed by varying the types of meats consumed, incorporating organ meats like liver, which are rich in vitamins A, D, E, and K, as well as B vitamins, and by choosing fatty fish for omega-3 fatty acids.

Digestive changes are also common, as the body adjusts to a higher intake of protein and fat, with a significant reduction in fiber. Some people may experience constipation or diarrhea initially. To support digestive health, it's important to balance fat and protein intake, consume bone broth for its gut-supportive properties, and gradually increase the amount of fat consumed to allow the digestive system to adapt.

Social and lifestyle adjustments represent another challenge, as dining out or attending social events can be difficult when adhering to such a restrictive diet. Planning ahead by reviewing restaurant menus or eating beforehand can help manage these situations. Additionally, explaining the health motivations behind choosing the carnivore diet can foster understanding and support from friends and family.

Finally, the mental challenge of restricting food variety should not be underestimated. The monotony of eating primarily meat can lead to boredom or cravings for forbidden foods. Experimenting with different cuts of meat, cooking methods, and allowable seasonings can help keep meals interesting and satisfying.

While the carnivore diet presents several challenges, particularly during the initial transition, understanding these hurdles and implementing strategic solutions can greatly enhance the likelihood of success and long-term adherence. It's also advisable for individuals to consult with healthcare professionals before and during their dietary transition to ensure their nutritional needs are met and to monitor any health changes.

Tips for Overcoming Dietary Hurdles

Adopting a carnivore diet involves a significant shift from the typical dietary patterns that include a variety of plant-based foods. This transition can present numerous challenges, from managing cravings for carbohydrates and sugars to ensuring nutritional adequacy and dealing with social dining situations. One of the first hurdles many encounters is the craving for sugars and carbohydrates, deeply ingrained from previous eating habits. A practical solution is to gradually decrease carb intake before fully transitioning to the carnivore diet, allowing the body to adjust. Additionally, consuming high-fat cuts of meat can help satiate cravings by providing a sense of fullness and satisfaction.

Another common challenge is ensuring a balanced intake of nutrients, given the limited food variety. To address this, focusing on a diverse range of animal-based foods, including organ meats, fish, eggs, and dairy (if tolerated), can provide a wide spectrum of essential nutrients, vitamins, and minerals. Organ meats, in particular, are nutrient-dense and can help prevent deficiencies.

Social situations and dining out can also pose significant challenges, as many social events revolve around food choices that are not carnivore-friendly. A useful strategy is to plan ahead by checking restaurant menus for suitable options or suggesting dining locations that offer simple, meat-based dishes. When attending social gatherings, bringing your own carnivore-approved foods can ensure you have something to eat without compromising your dietary choices.

Digestive adjustments to a meat-only diet can be uncomfortable for some, especially in the initial stages. To mitigate these issues, it's advisable to start with leaner meats and gradually increase fat intake, allowing the digestive system to adapt. Additionally, drinking plenty of water and incorporating bone broth can aid digestion and ease the transition.

Variety and boredom with food choices can become a challenge over time. Experimenting with different cuts of meat, cooking methods, and using minimal amounts of allowed seasonings can help keep meals interesting and enjoyable. Trying exotic meats or incorporating carnivore-friendly recipes can also introduce new flavors and textures, keeping the diet diverse and satisfying.

Lastly, the financial aspect of consuming high-quality animal products exclusively can be daunting for some. To manage costs, buying in bulk, choosing cuts of meat that are less expensive, and shopping for deals at local butchers or online meat suppliers can make the carnivore diet more affordable. Opting for frozen meats or purchasing directly from farmers are additional ways to save money without compromising on the quality of the diet.

By addressing these challenges with practical solutions, individuals following the carnivore diet can navigate dietary hurdles effectively, maintaining adherence to the diet while enjoying its health benefits.

Chapter 11: Health and Nutrition

Nutritional Benefits of a Carnivore Diet

The carnivore diet, focusing exclusively on animal products, offers a unique array of nutritional benefits that stem from its high protein, fat, and essential nutrient content. Rich in vitamins A, D, E, and K2, found abundantly in animal fats, this diet supports bone health, immune function, and cardiovascular health. The diet's emphasis on high-quality animal protein aids in muscle repair and growth, making it particularly beneficial for those looking to maintain or increase muscle mass.

One of the standout features of the carnivore diet is its provision of complete proteins. These proteins contain all nine essential amino acids necessary for the human body's functions, which plant-based proteins often lack in one or more. This aspect is crucial for the body's repair processes, hormonal balance, and enzyme production.

The carnivore diet is naturally low in carbohydrates, which can lead to a state of ketosis where the body becomes efficient at burning fat for energy instead of glucose. This shift has been associated with weight loss, improved insulin sensitivity, and a reduction in blood sugar levels, offering potential benefits for those with diabetes or metabolic syndrome.

Furthermore, the diet provides high levels of omega-3 fatty acids, particularly from fatty fish like salmon and sardines, which are known for their anti-inflammatory properties. These fatty acids contribute to brain health, reducing the risk of depression, and cognitive decline.

Another significant benefit is the high content of bioavailable iron found in red meat, crucial for preventing anemia. The heme iron in animal products is more easily absorbed by the body compared to non-heme iron found in plant sources.

The carnivore diet also simplifies nutrition by eliminating the need to track nutrient intake from various food sources, as animal products contain virtually all the nutrients the human body needs in bioavailable forms. This simplicity can lead to improved digestive health for some people, as the diet excludes fiber and plant-based substances that can irritate the gut in sensitive individuals.

Despite these benefits, it's important for individuals to consider the potential need for supplementation, such as vitamin C, which is lower in animal products. However, historical evidence suggests that in the absence of carbohydrates, the human body may require significantly less vitamin C, potentially reducing the concern for deficiency.

In summary, the carnivore diet offers a nutrient-dense approach to eating that emphasizes the consumption of whole animal products. It provides essential vitamins, minerals, fatty acids, and proteins in highly bioavailable forms, supporting a range of health outcomes from muscle maintenance and growth to improved metabolic health. As with any diet, individuals should consider their unique nutritional needs and potential adaptations to ensure a balanced approach to health and well-being.

Potential Risks and How to Mitigate Them

Embarking on a carnivore diet, which focuses exclusively on animal products and eliminates plant-based foods, can offer various health benefits such as weight loss, reduced inflammation, and improved blood sugar levels for some individuals. However, this diet also poses potential risks that require careful management to ensure overall health and nutritional balance.

One of the primary concerns with a carnivore diet is the risk of nutrient deficiencies. Animal products, while rich in proteins, fats, vitamins like B12 and minerals such as iron and zinc, lack other essential nutrients found in plants, including fiber, vitamin C, and certain antioxidants. To mitigate this risk, individuals can prioritize the consumption of organ meats, such as liver and kidney, which are packed with vitamins and minerals, including those typically sourced from plants.

Another risk is the potential increase in cholesterol and saturated fat intake, which may concern those with existing heart conditions or a family history of cardiovascular disease. Incorporating leaner meats and seafood can help manage fat intake, and regular monitoring of blood lipid levels with a healthcare provider can ensure that the diet does not adversely affect heart health.

The lack of dietary fiber in a carnivore diet could lead to digestive issues such as constipation. Consuming bone broth, which contains gelatin, can aid in digestive health by supporting the intestinal lining and promoting bowel movements. Additionally, staying well-hydrated and engaging in regular physical activity can help maintain digestive regularity.

There is also the concern of increased exposure to toxins and pollutants through high consumption of animal products, particularly if they come from non-organic sources. To reduce exposure to antibiotics, hormones, and pesticides, opting for grass-fed, pasture-raised, and organic meat sources when possible is advisable. This choice not only supports better health but also promotes more sustainable farming practices.

The environmental impact of a carnivore diet, primarily due to the high demand for meat, is another consideration. Choosing locally sourced and ethically raised animal products can help mitigate some of these environmental concerns by supporting farming practices that are more in harmony with nature and reduce the carbon footprint associated with long-distance food transport.

Social and practical challenges may also arise, as dining out and sharing meals with others can become more complicated. Planning ahead, selecting restaurants that offer suitable options, and communicating dietary preferences clearly can help manage these situations and maintain social connections.

Finally, the transition to a carnivore diet should be approached gradually, allowing the body to adjust to the new eating pattern. Starting with a balanced approach that includes a variety of animal-based foods and closely monitoring the body's response can help identify any potential issues early on. Regular check-ups with a healthcare provider to monitor health markers and nutritional status are crucial to ensure that the diet supports overall health.

In summary, while the carnivore diet can offer health benefits for some, it also comes with potential risks that require careful consideration and management. Through strategic food choices, monitoring health markers, and making adjustments as needed, individuals can address these concerns and pursue a carnivore diet that supports their health and nutritional needs.

Conclusion

In wrapping up the discussion on the carnivore diet and its associated food list, it's clear that this diet represents a radical departure from conventional dietary guidelines which typically advocate for a balanced intake of both animal and plant-based foods. The carnivore diet, with its focus solely on animal products, offers a unique perspective on nutrition and health, underscored by testimonials and anecdotal evidence from its proponents who report significant health improvements. These benefits range from weight loss and enhanced mental clarity to the alleviation of autoimmune symptoms and reduced inflammation.

However, the journey through a carnivore diet is not without its challenges and potential health risks. Nutrient deficiencies, changes in cholesterol levels, digestive issues, and the environmental impact of high meat consumption are concerns that require thoughtful consideration and management. The diet demands a commitment to not only consuming a variety of animal products, including organ meats and seafood, to maintain nutritional balance but also a readiness to monitor and adapt to the body's responses over time.

Moreover, the diet emphasizes the importance of quality in the selection of animal products. Opting for grass-fed, pasture-raised, and organic options can mitigate some of the health and environmental concerns associated with the carnivore diet. Such choices support more sustainable agricultural practices and reduce exposure to harmful substances, aligning with a more conscientious approach to consumption.

Adopting a carnivore diet also invites a reflection on the social and practical aspects of eating. It challenges individuals to navigate dining out, social gatherings, and family meals with a restrictive dietary pattern, fostering creativity and openness in dietary choices and communication.

Ultimately, the carnivore diet underscores a broader dialogue about health, nutrition, and the role of individual dietary choices in promoting wellness. It serves as a reminder of the diversity in human nutrition, the adaptability of the human body, and the ongoing quest for optimal health through diet. Whether one chooses to embrace the carnivore diet in its entirety, incorporate aspects of it, or pursue a different nutritional path, the key lies in informed, mindful eating practices that support one's health goals and lifestyle.

As research continues to evolve, so too will the understanding of the carnivore diet and its place within the spectrum of dietary options available to those seeking to optimize their health. The conversation around the carnivore diet, rich with both enthusiastic support and cautious skepticism, reflects the complexity of nutrition science and the personal nature of dietary choice. It remains an intriguing area for further study and exploration, highlighting the need for a nuanced approach to diet that considers individual variability, health objectives, and the holistic impact of food choices on well-being and the environment.

30 Days Meal Plan

Day	Breakfast	Lunch	Dinner
1	Scrambled eggs	Grilled salmon fillet	Beef steak
2	Sardines in olive oil	Tuna salad (mayonnaise optional)	Pork chops
3	Omelets with bacon	Mackerel fillets	Chicken thighs
4	Hard-boiled eggs	Smoked salmon slices	Lamb chops
5	Salmon patties	Grilled sardines	Ribeye steak
6	Tuna steak	Bacon-wrapped scallops	Beef liver
7	Deviled eggs	Sardine salad	Turkey breast
8	Smoked mackerel	Tuna and avocado salad	Pork ribs
9	Salmon and cream cheese rolls	Mackerel pate	Chicken wings
10	Egg muffins	Sardines with lemon	Beef kebabs
11	Tuna omelet	Grilled salmon salad	Lamb shoulder
12	Bacon slices	Tuna steaks	Beef tenderloin
13	Salmon scramble	Sardine fillets	Pork belly
14	Smoked mackerel	Tuna and egg salad	Chicken

Day	Breakfast	Lunch	Dinner
	salad		drumsticks
15	Sardine omelet	Mackerel sushi rolls	Ribeye roast
16	Tuna salad	Grilled sardine skewers	Lamb burgers
17	Eggs and bacon	Salmon ceviche	Beef brisket
18	Mackerel scramble	Tuna steak with butter	Pork tenderloin
19	Sardine patties	Smoked salmon salad	Chicken skewers
20	Tuna avocado boats	Mackerel salad	Beef stir-fry
21	Bacon-wrapped eggs	Sardine pate	Lamb shanks
22	Salmon roe	Tuna salad wraps	Pork sausages
23	Mackerel and cream cheese	Grilled sardine fillets	Chicken thighs with skin
24	Tuna and cucumber salad	Smoked mackerel fillets	Beef ribs
25	Sardine scramble	Tuna avocado salad	Lamb chops
26	Salmon sushi rolls	Mackerel pate	Pork chops
27	Tuna melt	Grilled sardines with lemon	Chicken drumsticks
28	Bacon and eggs	Sardine salad	Beef tenderloin

Day	Breakfast	Lunch	Dinner
29	Smoked salmon and cream cheese	Tuna steak	Lamb kebabs
30	Mackerel ceviche	Sardine omelet	Pork belly strips

Made in United States
Troutdale, OR
10/29/2024